SONGS
from the
MIFFLINGER SEA
and a little cove of
NONSENSE

Allan W. Anderson

Illustrated by Leslie Rhea Lewis

AND GOD SAID.................

Let there be many-colored rainbows

And at the end of each a pot of gold

Let there be fairies to decorate the night

As the dragonflies decorate the day

Let there be tales told on a winter's night

While the fire sings and elves dance beneath the moon

Let there be sweets and foreign scented fruits

And as many toys as there are dewdrops at dawn

Let all these things be; sparing nothing

Neither sounds, nor colors, nor tastes, nor shapes

Nor anything needful...................

For the sake of a child

For Howard, Mary, Bruce and Kare.

Print information available on the last page

Rev. date: 01/29/2019

To order additional copies of this book, contact:
Xlibris
1-888-795-4274
www.Xlibris.com
Orders@Xlibris.com

Contents

A Tale From This Old Armchair

The twilight is falling, the world has grown still

Each bird has returned to her tree

And now is the time when the children all come

Running to look for me --

For a tale will be told from this old armchair

And a place is reserved on my knee.

Why do rabbits have soft long ears

And noses that twitch in the sun?

Or would centipedes really forget how to walk

If they counted their legs one by one?

But such questions can only be answered for sure

By a field mouse that's caught on the run.

So come let us hear a story or two

Tho' that's all I think I can share

Till I catch that old field mouse again on the run

That mouse with his nose in the air

And when the tales are all ended you'll soon fall asleep

Safe asleep in the cove of my care.

I

THE MIFFLINGER SEA

The Mifflinger Sea

By the sea,
By the ancient Mifflinger Sea
Where the whale and the herring sport amiably
Let us go down, down over the lea
To the emerald waters of the Mifflinger Sea.

Great gentle beasts romp the night sand
Chasing the line between water and land,
While exquisite peacocks, in step three by three,
Watch pompously down by the Mifflinger Sea.

Tiny blue shells glow on the shore
Like shimmering moons, and some cup the door
To intricate passages used by strange wee
Inhabitants of the Mifflinger Sea.

I have recently come from this Ocean whose vast
Waters encompass all Future, all Past
They draw from a stream whose deeps ever remain
The font of our pleasure, the ebb of our pain.

By the sea,
By the ancient Mifflinger Sea
Where the whale and herring sport amiably
Let us go down, down over the lea
To the emerald waters of the Mifflinger Sea.

The Land Where the Pom-Poms Grow

What of the land
The fabulous land
Where the bashful Pom-poms grow
Beneath giant trees a-swirl in the breeze
Over rainbows asleep in the snow.

The Pom-poms are seen
When a moon-tinted sheen
Lights the banks of a river so large
It takes fifty years and twenty-one tears
To cross on a rudderless barge.

You may go to the land
The fabulous land
Where the bashful Pom-pom grows,
If you ring the bluebell
Twice as thin as a shell
Which was lost by the King of the Snows.

Has he been there before?
Oh! A thousand times more
For he lives on the banks of that stream
Where the shy Pom-poms peep at the rainbows asleep
On the rim of a winter-night's dream
Yes, the rim.
On the rim of a winter-night's dream.

Ludo Bay

Where the rocks reach to the waters
Of the ancient Ludo Bay
A Penguin stands attending
In a most impressive way
Stands attending and defending
One new timeless Ludo day

And the flocks of feathered porters
Sauntering up and down the Bay
Think not once to question
His most odd impressive way
For none dares raise the question
That reversed one Ludo day

It was not so altogether
Down in ancient Ludo Bay
A smaller Penguin tending
In a less impressive way
Found just the very ending
To one timeless Ludo day

And the flocks of feathered porters
Sauntering up and down the Bay
Did hear him ask the question
In his less impressive way
Heard him ask the fated question
That reversed the Ludo day

For it was so altogether
Down in ancient Ludo Bay
Till smaller Penguin tending
In his less impressive way
Did ask whose egg was bending
In a most unusual way

And the birds, the feathered porters
Sauntering up and down the Bay
Gazed each upon the other
In a most disdainful way
No bird might stay in Ludo
Who laid eggs some other way!

Still the rocks reach to the waters
Of the ancient Ludo Bay
Old Penguin stands attending
In his most impressive way
Who would never think of ending
This new timeless Ludo day.

How the Pobbles Came to the Sea

There are Peebles that live by the shoreline
Unheard, unseen, unknown
But Young Pebbles insist they have seen them
Though Peebles are not made of stone

Now the old Pebbles called a great meeting
To decide whether Peebles could be
They resolved "We deny the existence
Of aught but The Stone and The Sea"

But Young Pebbles are wiser than wisdom
And their eyes are cleaner than flame
They continue the mention of Peebles
Disregarding the Old Pebbles shame

God's help for the proper old Pebbles!
For a tale is all over the lea
Young Pebbles and Peebles are pibbling
Of a new Pobble who sits by the sea

How Margaret McMuffin Came to the Sea

Margaret McMuffin

A young lady I know,

Owns a Pink Puffin

She walked in the snow;

She walked quite about

Above and below

Did Margaret McMuffin

With her Puffin in snow

Margaret McMuffin

Out of pure pleasure,

Taught her Pink Puffin

To dance a quaint measure.

Then maidens full stout,

Some tall and quite fair

Danced Margaret's poor Puffin

Into despair.

Margaret McMuffin

With tears and sore groans,

Watched her Pink Puffin

Fall, tatters and bones.

She snatched him away

And wrenched herself free

And came with her Puffin

To the Mifflinger Sea.

Margaret McMuffin

A young lady of yore,

Owns a Pink Puffin

She walks by the shore -

They idle about

And visit the lea

McMuffin and Puffin

Of the Mifflinger Sea

My Fountain

"I have a fountain in my garden"

I said to a little bird one day

Then he replied, "I beg your pardon

But just what was it I heard you say?"

"I have a fountain in my garden"

I repeated to him as before

"Oh," he answered, "I beg your pardon.

Pray, what is your fountain for?"

"My fountain plays for my delight

A silver melody

And sparkles in the evening light

Like crystal jewelry."

"Oh," said the little bird again

"I see what I must do"

And flew to the fountain's edge and then

He sang the whole night through.

And sometimes when I wake at night

And listen carefully

The brown bird sings with all his might

His silver melody.

And then I think of what I've heard

And dream. I dream of what, did you say?

Why, I dream of a little brown bird who sings

Where my silver fountains play.

The Golden Ring

In the days when the mouse was small as a pea

And angels walked among men

There came a lad to the Mifflinger Sea

With a pup, a string, and a hen

The pup, he played with the string all day

And the boy swam far in the sea

While the hen, she laid a thoughtful egg

So quiet and amiably

And the egg, it hatched to a full grown song

In the shape of a moon-gold maid

Who tied the pup to the string and the boy

And the shell the hen had laid

And then the girl and the bird began

To bind themselves to the three:

The shell, the pup and the boy that came

To the ancient Mifflinger Sea

And these five that came to the sea to stay

They move by an infinite string

That draws them each to the other's play

Around love's golden ring.

The Lost Loon

"I would caution you now"

Said the elegant Foon

"I would caution you never to dine

While roses are blowing

And quiet tears are flowing

Around the island of June"

"I must go just the same"

Said the fierce-feathered Loon

"I must go where the sorrowful air

Balloons on a stubble

Until the great bubble

Reflects the magical Rune"

So he went on his way

Disregarding the Foon

And he came while the Roses of Care

Leaned languidly blowing

Toward tears quietly flowing

Around the island of June

"I can't stay very long"

Said the fierce-feathered Loon

"I'll just wait till the sorrowful air

Balloons on a stubble

And then on that bubble

I'll read the magical Rune"

He forgot what was said

By the elegant Foon

And he dined while the Roses of Care

Perfumed all their blowing

Toward tears quietly flowing

Around the island of June

On the very next day

While the fierce-feathered Loon

Made a path through the sorrowful air

He found a small stubble

That grew a wee bubble

But not the magical Rune

"I had cautioned him though"

Says the elegant Foon

"See, he's lost in the Roses of Care

And bubbles he's blowing

From tears quietly flowing

Around the island of June"

The Marbo

The Marbo has said

"I want for my bed

A pumpkin that's sliced into three

So all through the night

We may sail out of sight

My self, my shadow, and me."

The Womrath replied

"Your mother has cried

To think you should leave her so soon

And sail far away

Where the green turtles play

And bubble their sighs to the moon."

But the Marbo still said

"I want for my bed

A pumpkin that's sliced into three

So all through the night

We may sail out of sight

My self, my shadow, and me."

Space Song

When the bleeps and bloops had blipped their blame

And the ocean lapped the shoal of shame,

The Buggit, the Boffle and Terrence McGhee

Cavorted beside the Mifflinger Sea

Roared the Boffle, "Ye gods! the Wombat, look - !"

Mashing the air with an urgent book,

Wombat squealed, "Boffle, Buggit, Terrence McGhee

It's over and done, she's feathered and free."

Boffle sighed long and pulled on his ears

The Buggit blinked, McGhee shed five tears

For the Wombat proclaimed with voice grave and thin,

The moon was feathered and freed from chagrin

Then the Wombat wheezed how earthlings fell

From the Moon and flopped into space pell-mell

For the Mippets had fashioned her wings that tall

She flapped and shook rockets, spacemen and all.

She may bathe and glide not far from shore

While the Mippits swoop all around her, for

The Buggit, the Boffle and Terrence McGhee

Stand Moon-Guard beside the Mifflinger Sea

The Self

Noobar MacNumpkin the prophet

Moutheth great things, bold and bare;

He boometh, "Come forth!" and "Come off it!""

He hideth a newt in his hair.

He straighteneth a slippery noodle –

Measureth it from his nose to his knee;

He nourisheth himself on this foodle:

"None beareth true tidings but me."

Who laugheth and spitteth at Noobar

Hath lost the old game of the pea;

Whether underling, thou, or a poohbah –

MacNumpkin undoes thee and me.

Her Fussness

From the Bumphorous Woods the Puss-Pet came

Her tail quite high in the breeze

Her fussness had heard all fish were quite tame

That swam in the Mifflinger Sea.

Yet she barely had set her face toward shore

Her eyes gold-green with delight

When something brushed past one delicate paw

That gave her a terrible fright

Then she stopped to examine this sight.

Toward the Bumphorous Woods did Puss-Pet churn

Her tail quite low in the breeze

She vowed she will never ever return

Insulted, she swears she never will turn

Her face toward the Mifflinger Sea.

II

DAYS WHEN WE WERE VERY SMALL

Those days when we were very small

Before the Real was dreamed

The wonders met were plainly known

To be just what they seemed

Blue Flower

I emptied a blue flower

After her shower

As we had arranged you know,

For the rain had filled up

Almost all of her cup

And made her too heavy to grow.

Pansy

This pansy is the queerest flower,

It has a face so long and sour,

But if I turn to look and pause,

The pansy laughs like Santa Claus.

Black Bird

Black bird, black bird

Sitting on a tree

Fly away, fly away -

One! Two! Three!

Fly to the mountains,

Tell Old King Snow

To wake up from slumber

And make the winds blow.

For I have a boat

And I have a kite

But I need a stiff wind

To blow them aright.

Black bird, black bird

Sitting on a tree,

Fly away, fly away -

One! Two! Three!

Dream a Little

Dream a little, just a little

As the clouds float by,

Where they float to no one knows,

So big and wide is the sky.

When I return from the land of NOW

I'll say to my friend, Bill,

And as I watch them sailing by,

They seem like ships, from where I lie.

"Come sail away on my cloud for a day,

We shall play whatever we will."

Someday I shall sail a cloud

And sit upon its prow;

Then sail away across the sky

To the land that's known as NOW.

Dream a little, just a little

As the clouds float by;

And one's a ship that's all my own

To sail the wide blue sky.

For in the land of NOW, they say

There is no THEN, or WHEN

You only play what's fun right now

Then play it over again.

Bumble Bee

Did you ever wonder

Did you ever care

What makes a bumble bee

Fly through the air?

All the school teachers

And all the wise men

Cannot tell, yet he flies

Again and again.

Did you ever wonder

Did you ever care

How heavy bumble bees

Fly through the air?

Fairy Fantasy

Tinkle, twinkle, tinkle, twinkle,

Here the fairies come;

Lightly skipping, lightly tripping

Dancing to some elfin air ----

Bells a-tinkle, wands a-twinkle

Crystal tinsel everywhere.

Tiny green elves amuse themselves

Riding balloons of thistle down;

Wafted nowhere, fancy free

Fluting a fairy fantasy.

Wrinkled gnomes sweep toadstool homes

With brooms made of fly legs and floss;

While centipede knaves,

The fairies' slaves,

Are mowing soft lawns of moss.

Tinkle, twinkle, pixies sprinkle

Dewdrops in the perfumed night.

Moonbeams quiver, dewdrops shimmer,

Glowworms glimmer their delight

As floating feather-like into sight

The fairy queen appears

She waves a wand of silver light

The crickets raise their cheers

And hail the magic in her hand

That turns the world to Fairyland.

Pixie Play

Far away, far away, over the sea

A little bird sometimes calls to me

He tells me of all the strange places he's known

Of the wonderful countries through which he has flown --

It's all a great secret, and I'm almost sure

That he'd really not mind if I mentioned one tour

Which he took through a truly remarkable land

That is ruled by an Elf and his Green Pixie band;

And these Pixies are all a mischievous folk

Who love impish fun and a practical joke.

As you know, hens will set on their eggs through the day

Well, at night time these Pixies will steal eggs away

And take them to places they've specially made

For hatching wee chicks in their magical glade.

Now when the chicks hatch in their bright yellow fluff

These Pixies get ready to make a bright muff;

They take bits of down from each baby chick --

Of course not too much, lest the chick should get sick --

But enough, to be sure, for all they may need

And each Pixie sews with a tiny green reed.

They sew night and day, and when they have done

All scamper away for even more fun.

They take the muff with them to place on a lawn

Near where pink butterflies sometimes are born,

Then each hides behind a fresh blade of grass

And watches to see the butterflies pass.

Well, this one I'll tell you of, lingered so near

The Pixies kept quiet lest she overhear.

She hovered above the bright yellow thing

And then tried to fit it right over her wing.

But somehow she just couldn't manage at all

And soon she was caught in the bright yellow ball.

And then the Green Pixies sprang forward with glee

And cried, "Stupid Butterfly! Why can't you see

You're lovely enough with your beautiful wings

And you don't need to wear any more gorgeous things?

But because you're so stupid and silly and vain

We're going to change you back again

A caterpillar again you shall be

A wooly one, yellow one, One Two! Three!"

So that's what became of the poor butterfly

And now she just crawls and looks at the sky.

Now maybe whenever you're humming a song

And a caterpillar happens along,

If you look very carefully perhaps you'll see

It's the one the Green Pixies changed magically.

Or should you ever find some soft thistle down

A bright yellow color like baby chick's down,

It could be a muff these Pixies have made

With a tiny green reed in their magical glade.

But what of these Chicks when the Pixies were gone?

Well, each baby Chick turned into a Swan!

Flower

There is a flower outside my window

It has grown quite tall

In the wind and the rain I really don't know

How it stands at all

Unless, of course, there are little people

Who watch flowers grow

And rush to help those thin as a steeple

While the gales blow.

32

III

A LITTLE COVE OF NONSENSE

Mozzling

While sitting within a Yummalong tree

Amid the pallid plains of Plohr

I mozed upon a surly bee

Who fuzzled there so shamefully

The sun sneaked round behind his core

To peep at how the moon forebore

This tiresome anomaly

A fuzzling drone

A mozzled me

Tender Tales

When tender tales and tuneful wails

Are wafted on a baleful sea

The fervid clams release their dams

And leave the world to you and me

Sir Roderick MacDewd

I say you look frightful said the Lellyman seal

With your earplug of sponge and three hairs

Have faith! quoth the old seadog Sir Roderick MacDewd

It saves me when floating around in the newd

From scaring wee crabs at their prayers

Shy Worm

It's a shocking bad thing, the worm declared,

To be sliced by two by three

I always end around the bend

And lose my modesty

The Gnome Traveler

There was a gnome who loved to roam

In summer, fall, and winter

But in the spring he took his fling

By floating on a splinter

The Presumptuous Fish

There was a fish who loved to swish

His tail in oysters' faces

But he strayed away

Where a giant clam lay

Who nipped off all further disgraces

The Plimptons of Plome

The Plimptons of Plome

Still shriek in their dome

With a badly behaved Northern loon

You may not address them

Nor see nor assess them

If you have but one tooth in your comb

The Plimpton's chief bane?

Fur tails in the rain

Or a barely inflated balloon

Their shrieking will wreck them

But no one can check them

Since they faint when advised to abstain

Old Man of Swyesevern

There was an Old Man of Swyesevern

Who said, "I'm a rip and a grethern!"

But others declared,

"He's a trifle too scared

And is only a pip in a blethern."

The Plimpton Dumbs

Plenty of plums for the Plimpton dumbs

Is the recipe most prescribed;

Though Algernon Pufferpate Brights M.D.

Improves it by adding a profligate pea

Twirled slowly between his paranoid thumbs --

It's by far the best thing for the Plimpton dumbs

McGoo

There is an old liar of Skidoo

Who keeps two sweet rolls in a shoe

He told them, he said

He would eat them instead!

What can an old fibber do?

This funny old fibber McGoo.

The Queen and the Bat

Have you heard of the Queen

Who turned purple green

When a bat flew under her chair?

She looked high and low

But the bat wouldn't show

Though she swore she would pull out her hair

She cried, "By my land

I'll pull out each strand

Till I'm bald as a bone in the sun."

But she's really quite wrong,

Though she pulls all day long

She will never get rid of her bun.

And the bat laughs all day

To hear the Queen say

"I'll do nothing but pull out my hair.

For I know where you're at

But because of my fat

I cannot reach under my chair."

IV

UNLEARNING WE'RE FULL GROWN

When the eye of childhood closes

We boast we walk alone –

A dream from which we waken,

Unlearning we're full grown

Hahna

The flowers of Caradeena

Like the birds of Trennacore

Recall the clouds of Hahna

Her caverns and her shore.

Her caverns and her shoreline

Sea-change the lost and blown--

A melt, a brew of mist-wine

Arises, heaven's own.

Birth-bold, the clouds of Hahna

Break water and outpour

The flowers of Caradeena

The birds of Trennacore.

Wander-lamb

Wander-lamb, Wander-lamb

Where are you roaming

Over the down and the lea?

Wander-lamb, Wander-lamb

Far in the gloaming

Wait, still wait for me

Wander-lamb, Wander-lamb

Where are you turning

Turning so lightly, so free?

Wander-lamb, Wander-lamb

Lord of unlearning

Light of care's elegy

Wander-lamb, Wander-lamb

All of our growing

Draws a slow tear from our glee

Wander-lamb, Wander-lamb

Round its clear flowing

Dance, still dance for me

The Charm

He came and sat upon my arm.

From his neck he took a charm

Stranger than a dream to see.

He handed it to me.

I saw the charm was strictly made

Of tears alternate with jade

Permanently now unwet --

A frozen alphabet.

Tarna

Near the stream of Tarna

Stone and flower combine—

Dapperlings and dandiprats

Are pressing petal wine

And these glen-green potions

Drawn through flutes of floss,

Elfin-quiet and fairy-fanned,

Mature in vats of moss

When the vale of Lóchan

Clasps the moon's pale horn

Silver-shadow dragon-flies

And leprechauns are born

Then the pool of Tarna

Plays her druid theme

Raising shades that flit and flare

Through Sleeping Beauty's dream

Lóchan: ch as in Scots loch

The Flowers of Chembuk Plain

In the fields of Chembuk Plain

A flower grows

In heaven knows

How many wanton shapes, delays,

To tease the wind out of his ways

The poopul bloom, the svarlip brush

The wozzle-tooth, the Krain-doh-luth

They congregate, conspire and craze

The clouds

On Mount Sha-moh-drigaze

The wailful winds and waters sleep

Unsound on that uncertain ground

Where flowers weave

The charmed sun's rays

Long sleeves to slow

His wheel of days

Then

In those days there came such sounds

As now I never hear

All songs that fall upon a child

Before he looks on fear

For then the whirr of tiny wings

The language of the leaves

Came fresh as whispers from the sea

When ocean heaves

In days when we were very small

And in that ageless long ago

Before the Real was dreamed

The wonders met were plainly known

To be just what they seemed.

V

THE MIFFLINGS' PASSING

The Mifflings' Passing

On the downs of Willow Wander

Near the stream of Pallinor

Sits a frail and sighing remnant

Of the race of Trennacore

The one, sole dying member

Of the race of Trennacore

Never mind how days were fonder

Of a light that shines no more

Never mind how night was fervid

For the gold the stars once wore

The gold with which each ember

Thrilled the night's dark corridor

Still she sits and weeps, far yonder,

For the Mifflings once of yore,

For the ancient race of Mifflings

And their crystal moon-washed shore,

Their misted smilings on her

Noble race of Trennacore

Once, as Mifflings paused to ponder

How the stream of Pallinnor

Uttered notes of unknown wisdom,

Came the birds of Trennacore

With wings of golden tincture

Crying; "No, not one song more!"

For the Mifflings ogled wonder

By the stream of Pallinnor

Gazed immodestly on wonder

In the realm of Trennacore

Till birds of lemulous number

Tore them, peeled them pore to core

Gone the Mifflings, sunken under

That strange stream of Pallinnor

Gone the misted moon-stroked marvels

With the race of Trennacore

Who mourned the Mifflings' passing

And their violet tinted shore

Still, one sits and weeps, far yonder,

For the Mifflings once of yore

Though their pause unbraced the rainbow

Round their crystal moon-washed shore

Drowned silver songs and broke her

Golden race of Trennacor

I once heard this sorrowed tale told

While wandering down the lea

As my mabbish, wild companion

Munched on flomes of neutered pea

We sang and sang our love songs

"O Mifflinger, Mifflinger, Mifflinger Sea!"

These are verses from the land of gentle light, the light that steals upon us unawares at dawn and eventide. Then the birds sing most lustily and the animals come together, friends and enemies alike, to the edge of that water from which they drink their life.

Nature gives us all a quiet space that lies between doing and not-doing. This, our true home, never binds nor casts us out. Ever able to leave it at will, we later find it cannot let us go.

Oftentimes, as we grow older, we are told that faith is nonsense. Still, a wise man once wrote that "later it may come back to us in the form that nonsense is faith."

A.W.A.

Printed in the United States
By Bookmasters